Exterminating Angels

Exterminating Angels

Poems by

Alan Catlin

Cover design by Shay Culligan
Cover art by Gene McCormick, *Booth*

ISBN: 978-1-63980-138-1

Kelsay Books
502 South 1040 East, A-119
American Fork, Utah 84003
Kelsaybooks.com

Acknowledgments

American Journal of Poetry: "Two Lane Blacktop"
Art Mag: "A Walk on the Wild Side"
Asylum Floor: "Live and Let Die"
Beatnik Cowboy: "la vie en rose," "Winter's Bones"
Big Hammers: "The Proposition," "Lilith"
Blue Collar: "Patriot Games"
Chiron Review: "American Psycho," "Snake Pit"
Clark Street Review: "The Crying Game," "Night Hawks"
Creativity Webzine: "Murder on the Orient Express," "Blue
    Yonder," "Diary of a Mad Housewife"
Dead Snakes: "Wild at Heart," "Urban Cowboy"
Dumpster Fire Press: "Exterminating Angel," "The Waitress,"
    "Death Becomes Her," "Naked Lunch," "The Wanderers,"
    "Lust for Life," "Rules of Attraction"
Home Planet News: "Body Heat"
Homestead Review: "Killer Klowns," "Napalm Sunset," "Born on
    the Fourth of July"
Inbetweenhangovers: "As I Lay Dying," "Bay City Bombers,"
    "The Counselor," "Exodus," "After the Rehearsal," "Drug
    Store Cowboy," "Look Homeward Angel," "Cabaret,"
    "Ironweed," "Portrait of a Lady," "Home of the Brave,"
    "Murder My Sweet," "The Quiet American," "Even Dwarfs
    Started Small," "The Passenger"
Lummox: "Sympathy for the Devil"
Main Street Rag: "The Family"
Ol' Chanty: "The Long Hot Summer"
Red Fez: "Big City, Bright Lights"
Rusty Truck: "The Doors," "Drowning Pool," "The Long Riders"
Sheila na gig: "The Sacrifice," "The Stepford Wives" (as "The
    Widows")
South Florida Poetry Review: "The Black Book (as "In the End")
Trailer Park Review: "The Hunger"

Trajectory: "Looking for Mr. Goodbar"
Up the River: "Pulp Fiction (2)," "Night to Remember"
Your One Phone Call: "Angel Heart," "The Girl with the Dragon
Tattoo," "Night of the Living Dead," "The Professionals"

Contents

3-Exterminating Angels

1-Pulp Fiction

Pulp Fiction

They liked classic rock 'n roll,
especially The Killer at the keyboard
hopped on So Co and underage girls,
did drive-bys instead of drive-ins,
coke in lines but not the fizzy kind
that comes in bottles and cans,
were into the eye for an eye,
Old Testament vengeance tour
but not into turning the other cheek,
understood the Solomon solution
of cutting someone in half to solve
a complex problem but not the Psalms of.
Had a heavy Chevy, cherry red ride
modified to motor, white walls and
a plastic jesus on the dash, a curl of
mardi gras love beads around the rear
view; liked surf music on the sound
around: Beach Boys and Ventures,
Del Shannon and The Searchers,
needles and pins on tape and in their
eyebrows and arms, eyes like marble suns
setting into a blood red sea.

Angel Heart

You might hear a voice like hers once,
maybe twice, in a lifetime and it would
always be by chance in some lowdown,
dragged out, roadside bar after a near death
experience in some primal woods place
involving a high-speed blowout, or
up-close and personal, with some jacklit
creature of the night, a kind of close
encounter of the worst kind, requiring
a rent-a-wreck to get from this no account
place to another one. This would be one of
those no tell motel nights, requiring more
than a few beverages to sooth the beating
heart, this close to rescue vehicles,
and from roadside to bedside gurney
services.

The only obstacle keeping her
from a lifetime recording contract with a
major label, and a one-way ticket to the
Rock 'n Roll/ Country Western Hall of Fame
would be at the bar, in worn filthy denims,
and a blue work shirt, with red scrolled lettering
on the left side pocket, and he would be
ordering shots of sour mash, he'd wash down
with Silver Bullets in cans, while he ignored
the show. After each dead soldier, he'd crumple
the can on the bar, leave it there, and no one
would object. He made it known that he thought
anyone who drank light anything, or beer out of

a glass, was a pussy and should be whipped with
barbed wire and run out of town. He would
say it such a way that it might have happened
more than once already and no one was eager to
see it again. But that voice. Oh, that voice, that sounded
like cheap whiskey, unfiltered cigarettes
and purebred sex, was beyond believing.
Left everyone, but the object of her lust,
transfixed as she sang "I Can't Get No Satisfaction"
low and sweet and in a minor key that would make
Cat Power cream in her jeans. Would make risking
a slow death on a wooden cross, sugar coated
and covered by fire ants, seem sublime after
an hour alone with her and nowhere else to go.

As I Lay Dying

The only reason he'd never
slept with his sister was that
his father never got around to
having another child.
Was like one of those Faulkner
backwoods characters, more
feral than human.
Started drinking his daddy's
Shine not long after he was
weaned and his momma ran
off to be anywhere other than
where the old man was.
Even as a kid, he could shoot
anything you could put shells in
and rarely miss.
Only thing he liked more than
killing was, skinning.
Liked the feel of an animal's guts,
still warm and slimy, sliding through
his fingers and leaving a bloody
mess behind.
Graduated from varmints, squirrels,
and rabbits to coons and bucks.
Loved to lean in close as they died
to watch the lights inside go off.
Must have been imprinted on the eyes
of a dozen dead animals as the last thing
they'd seen before they went to
another place, before he reached the
age of seventeen.
Dreamed of what it would be like
to kill a man.

How it would feel to field dress one
and leave him hanging by his feet
until he had bled out.
Never thought about what might
happen to him after.
Was like those Faulkner folks
bearing the rotting corpse of their
momma, in a pine box, lost in
the woods in mid-summer looking
for a place they would never find,
more dead than alive themselves.

Casino

Whatever happened to all those hip
young people in TV ads for casinos?
You know the ones, the people who
are all starry eyed, and focused, hyper
and happy as hell, usually some young
studly with two hot blondes in skimpy
evening gowns, placing bets, rolling
dice, taking a hit, and celebrating:
"Yes, this is the life when you're high,
Addicted, and well paid!" What other
message could you possibly come
away with? As they skip down the green
carpeted, attached hotel complex hallways,
in this timeless place with no windows,
no clocks, nothing that suggested any place
but here, or an exact replica of here,
somewhere else. Like a reverse image
Dorothy in an Ozworld at the end of
the rainbow after all the gold has been
stolen by the people at the monitors in their
24/7 observation control rooms. After
the exhilaration of the tables, the floor show
of some gaudy, glitzy, formerly well-known
something or another, still high on unlimited
booze and speed, this magical trio retires
to their room/suite for some enthusiastic
three-way sex, on camera, to be sold later
as a hedge against losses at the tables
under the title Foxy Woods because sex
always sells. Even thirty years later,
the videos can be download because,
well, debauchery never gets old, even

after the performers do. They who are
now so far past their prime, they have
begun, second, even third careers, as
bona fide senior citizens, after movie work
dried up, and the rehab stints, and they
moved on to anonymity somewhere else
where they are less likely to be remembered
for what they looked like naked and in bed.
She the lady in buckskins, and leathers,
and the most incredible platinum wig ever
outside of a picture window, playing electronic
slots at a UK, M-Road rest stop, losing all
their mad money, while he is in the stalls
taking an epic, slow dump, too long there
to prevent the inevitable, another lost weekend
drinking tall boy Tennent's Lager by the seaside,
smoking Players and wondering where
it all went wrong.

The Crying Game

"There's nothing quite like being
a cop for the MTA. I was up in
The Bronx for the first six months,
talk about a bunch of losers!
It was like being in a War Zone
for hard time drug abusers.
I busted two guys the first day out
with about 36 vials of crack apiece,
some high bred skag, a couple of bags
of angel dust and enough grass to
turn on most of PS 169. The scary part
was they claimed it was for personal
use and no one disbelieved them.
I wonder what they're going to be like
if and when they get old enough to
know a little better, like 17.
Now I'm doing Manhattan which is pure
cake compared to that. I pulled down
some totally buzzed out geek just outside
of Times Square. He started out like
he was prepared to give me some serious
psycho shit so I laid one of my better
comedy lines on him, 'I understand
you're frustrated. I'm frustrated too.
Sometimes it makes me just feel like
killing someone, you know what I mean?
I'll bet right now, you'd like to say
something like, I'd love to see you dead,
getting zipped into a body bag, wouldn't you?
Go ahead, say it, it'll make you feel better.'
Asshole said it. Hello Bellevue. Got him
on a psycho charge, weeks of tests, rubber

rooms, the whole nine yards, and ain't no one
going to believe some deranged, criminally
insane person with a rap sheet longer than
the Declaration of Independence, that I put
him up to it. Best part about the whole gig
is no paperwork for yours truly. Ruined that
guys' life Big Time but what the hell,
it's just all part of the crying game, isn't it?"

The Quiet American

No more Boodles in a bottle
when the gin was gone, all the songs
ended, the movie credits snuffed out
like a certain kind of film, all the false
cheer dispersed into hangovers and
half-drunk raves leaving behind nothing
but the rank smell of cigarette ashes
and alcohol spills, broken glass and
squashed fruit on thrown rugs beyond
repair. In the after-haze, lying on stained,
yellow with sweat sheets, immobile in
the dehydrating heat, loose limbed and
thirsty for more, always more than there
is to drink, body bloat and tremoring limbs
at false dawn, fire ants devouring his
permanently scarred red eyes, more
than half-dead, listening to the insistent
click of the rotating fans dividing the air
into wounds.

Wild at Heart

The sleeves on his arms
suggested an intense, up close
and personal, history of violence.
A tale, no doubt, continued on parts
of his body covered by filthy clothes
stained by rough riding oil slick roads,
sleeping where he collapsed after
imbibing a quarter keg of beer and
enough Ketamine to fell a pair of
wild Bronc riders in a Texas prairie
dust storm. The tapestry in ink on his
back told of exploits only a trained
psychotic killer could hope to replicate.
The pictography read like a Russian
mafia skin job, a life story of a man
who found himself somehow transported
from the steppes into a clan of far west
America clan of skinheads. Decided he
liked their team ethic and core values
as they closely matched his own.
Was accepted as a walking recruitment
poster for limited IQ, wannabe bad asses
with identity issues who were virtually
useless on their own, but valuable as
contributing members of a pack.
Could channel a lifetime of hate for all
those people not of his kind, and translate
it into astonishing acts of extreme violence.
Claimed he would try the bullet trick with
live ammo at the next biker cook if
he didn't put his bike down at a hundred per.

Rode like his helmet was a shaped tin can
EMT's could use to put his brains in once
he popped his skull. A memorial of beer cans,
animal skulls, and spare parts from wrecked
rides mark where he left the road for good.

Bay City Bombers

They were the women's beer league
champions four years running.
Most were built like Bay City Bombers
after Raquel had left the team, all, that is
except for the pitcher, short fielder, and
second baseman, all of whom looked
like pixie dusted vestal virgins but were
known to scream like harlots when their
men went down hard where it mattered.
The MVP was part Calamity Jane,
part Blaze Starr, an authentic bad momma
who liked to play softball while the sun
shone and hard ball all night after post-game
parties. "I'm the MVP all right," she liked
to say in between shots of Ole, "Most
Valuable Pussy. "Made the police blotter,
the six o'clock news, and the DWI Hall of Fame
all in one night, driving so far over the limit
she was medically dead. Created a drive-in
door and window, totaling a car, and a Stewart's
Convenience store, in one go. Was quoted
as saying, after the EMT's scoped her for
obvious signs of injury, "I never felt a thing."

Live and Let Die

In his dreams, the women all
have porn star names: Monica Mayhem,
Lexxi Love, Victoria Sin. All of them
ached for his He Man body, though in
real life, he resembled Oliver Hardy
after a week's long Roman feast that
the emperor Nero would have enjoyed.
Thought beer, Cheetos, and nacho chips
with a synthetic product like cheese
was fine dining. After the repast,
he savored packs of generic menthols
he lit one from the other. The only known
exercise he got was lifting the remote,
pressing buttons and extended coughing
fits that anyone with final stage emphysema
could identify with. Was headed for one
of those operations where they remove
the voice box and replace it with an
electronic device you could use to order
take out with, on speaker phones.
Was destined to be the kind of guy
who smoked through a blow hole in
his throat and bitched because he could
no longer do double smoke rings to
impress the ladies. Such as they were.
Wouldn't be kidding when he wanted
to know why they couldn't put bourbon in
his glucose drip when it came to intravenous.
People began asking him what it was like
to die as if he'd ever been alive.

Nighthawks

The place where they drank,
suffused in shadows, fog and smoke,
more like opening scenes of "The Killers"
than a "Clean Well-Lighted Place",
more a graveyard scene than a primary,
Hopper colored, city night.
Local hoods in nearby burned out
storefronts, grinding broken plate
glass beneath shit kicker boots,
smoking skunk weed and drinking
warm malt liquor from paper bags
they will use later to start arson fires
just to watch the block burn.
Contract hit man drinking coffee
sludge from chipped diner cup waiting
for the Swede he came to kill or a text
message that directs him where to go
next, who to kill, or not, it doesn't matter
who or where, the coffee tastes the same.
Dead on her feet waitress in triple shift
soiled clothes, eyes swollen from lack of
sleep or hits of speed or both, feeling
the weight of too many days and nights
working a never closes café, one unfiltered
cigarette away from a fatal disease.
Walking health code violation head chef
and chief bottle washer, three quarters
of the way through a bottle a day habit
and nothing else to look forward to.
All of them waiting, waiting for the
mortuary van to come.

The Long Hot Summer

Still nights raw with heat
and the scent of spilled gasoline.
The ground so dry it aches for
rain that never comes.
Even the weeds dying, all the tall
grasses brown and seer like straw.
Nothing moves but beer drunk
youths, their thin torsos slick
with pitch and sweat, Zippo lighters
ready to crisp another wood
framed barn, to torch another field
just to watch the flames, the smoke
smother yet another hunter's moon.
Their feral eyes are as red as coals
that have absorbed all available light.

Killer Klowns (from Outer Space)

Heat struck and ill at ease.
Physically, inert, four quarts of beer
into a vicious, skunk beer drunk.
Vertigo spin of smoke, smog, and still,
humid air it hurts to breathe.

Inside, box fans slow the descent into maelstrom
to a slow crawl. Quells the bottle rocket's red
glare that stains the rancid sticky night.

The dead weight of the TV remote and the white
noise, the fever glow emanations from the wide
screen, morphing into a SYFY feature in progress.
Something involving human-sized aliens in clown
suits, beyond incredible to behold. Squeeze
the tempting red nose at your peril and suffer the
dread consequences later. Plot lines suggest
the suits are the actual extraterrestrial forms
these things-that-came-from-wrecked-space-ships
inhabit. Makes the casual, immobile, observer
wonder if the makers of domestic, three ring circus
brews, are lacing their product with acid in heavily
carbonated, liquid form. If true, imagine the leap
in sales to stratospheric heights beyond anyone's
reasonable expectation. Imagine aliens inhabiting
the earth and how no one notices and the ones
that do, don't care.

Even Dwarfs Started Small

After some kind of Children's Crusade
had gone horribly awry,

after all the leaders has been butchered
or driven into the wilderness, crosses pinned
to their bleeding backs,

after the asylum doors are opened and all
the stunt-growth children had matured,
grown old in body and mind but not in stature,
all of them undersized and driven mad by
privation, extreme lack of food and of water,
and forced to sleep nearly naked in all kinds
of weather until even a home for the deranged
seemed like paradise reclaimed,

after all the doctors, nurses, attendants had been
deposed, the one who sits in the director's chair
is king, is empowered to makes his subjects
march about the ravaged, asylum grounds
bearing wooden crosses with wild monkeys
affixed to them as Christ figures in la la land,

after the laughing prophet, tethered to a patient's
interview chair, is chastised, brow-beaten, reviled,
made to endure primitive recording sessions,
reel upon reel of hysterical laughter replayed
through speaker systems unedited for hours after
lights out,

after the still-functioning-vehicles are set in perpetual,
circular motion, all the landlines cut, the director
overthrown by the inmates, then hoisted on his
hard wood chair to where all the kindled wood
is burning,

after all this, the devil's prayers are answered,
his words chanted in broken phrases from
the original Aramaic, the second coming
of the Evil One is evoked and he comes tarnished
jesus eyes alight like fallen stars in a festering night.

The Passenger

They looked like a couple who'd spent
a weekend that was supposed to be
like "Breakfast at Tiffany's" but ended up
as "Last Tango in Paris." Driving down
narrow roads like wide lane thoroughfares
in top-down rental paid for with stolen ID
credit cards with no place in mind as good
as a destination with a double bed in it.
His arms dealer eyes are affixed on nothing,
hers on what can only be seen in rear view
mirrors. Nothing is certain where they are
headed, where they have been like Alphaville
in white, gun slits and turrets in the walls
instead of windows. Instead of a bouquet
of red roses, he supplies sticks of butter,
destination maps with no co-ordinates,
and a false key to mislead even the most
intrepid seekers after truth. The moving
pictures of their lives diverge even where
they intersect. The one who dies is a figment
of someone's fever dream, the other is a
passenger in a car.

Under the Volcano (2)

The man who walks straddles two worlds,
embracing neither, though spirit lamps
light the way. Skulls to honor the dead are
fashioned from sugar and sweetmeats are
served cold the way they were intended to be.
After feasts are consumed, fireworks are lit,
Roman candles explode overhead and torches
are carried by revelers climbing, single file,
up the narrow path to the lips of a volcano,
dormant for generations but still virile
in the minds of the people who worship there.
The man who walks had no god except the one
who resides inside a clear bottle disguised
as a worm whose wrinkled flesh can be consumed
but no wisdom is imparted. Even walking,
the man is insensible but has an uncanny
sense of balance and control, even after he has
completely lost his way. Wide awake yet dreaming,
he imagines the pianist's severed hands squeezing
his throat shut, obstructing the passages, blinding
all sight. Although this final movie is a silent one
and without color, the ending is not, torch light
precedes him but darkness envelops.

Blue Yonder

They bring things that are
of no use, not to them,
not to you, not to anyone:
broken ray guns, death star
storm trooper masks, tricorders
for contacting spaceships long
ago taken out by Vulcan war
ships, cracked hoses, watering
cans with no spouts, a Zen Garden
rake, all this stuff they want to
pack into the overloaded truck,
the space where the back seat
should be, all that junk lifted
from landfills and roadside attraction
dumps. A pry bar would be useful
for arranging latest acquisitions but
none are available at any price,
still the collecting goes on, after dark
by the lights of their short circuiting
dashboard, control panels, the static
from their radio broadcasting secret
messages from the wild blue yonder,
up there, where the stars are.

The Counselor

He looked like a body double for the original
Incredible Hulk gone to seed.
Wore a not quite large enough XXL
orange T-shirt that said:
"Florida the Gunshine State", on the front,
and "Shoot 'em as you see 'em" on the back.
Had a chewed-to-mush stogie in the left
corner of his mouth near the scar he got
calling a Cubano drug runner, a wetback
greaser in a bar in Miami. A man had to have
a serious death wish, or a posse large enough
to talk down the James Gang, to survive that…
Used to stub out a lit cigar on his forehead
to impress women he wanted to sleep with,
or dealers he did business with once, and once
only, to show how tough he was, and impervious
to pain, a trick that came off as something
only a seriously deranged person would attempt.
This too had its advantages.
That is, until the scarring got so bad,
grown men blanched when they got close
enough to see what he had done to himself.
Whores began charging him double just to be
alone with him, triple if he got near enough
for their lips to touch.
Didn't have a personality so much as a series
of traits that ranged all the way from vicious to
cruel and everything in between.
Would have looked perfect, if he lived long
enough, outfitted with that metal collar that
got applied to the neck of Brad Pitt as a sleazy
shyster in that Cormac McCarthy scripted flick,

that collar that was a self-tightening, vice like iron maiden thing, that gradually squeezed the life out of the wearer, severing the head from the body, as it clicked shut.

A Walk on the Wild Side

"He used to be someone I knew
but now he's someone else." Bukowski

The best way to describe what was
sitting in the last row of the express bus
to nowhere was, human garbage: close
cropped clumps of gray hair last cut
by monkeys with straight edges,
kitchen help duds stained by years
of grime and grease removed from fast
cooked food and smelling like it,
eyes rolled all the way back in his
perpetually nodding off eyes, so unhealthy
looking, so thin, he appeared to be in his
late forties going on dead. The only sign
of life beyond his apparel and the faint
movement of his convex caved chest,
was a wrinkled Daily Racing Form clutched
in the talon like fingers of his right hand.
No one was sitting within two rows of
where he was reclined despite standing room
only, rush hour crowd, just in case whatever
it was he had proved to be contagious,
though they need not have worried,
what he had was self-inflicted and fatal
but not something you could catch unless
you wanted to, had the cash to lay down
for another lid, another blast of smack,
that would hit so hard the rest of his teeth
would fall out.

Urban Cowboy

We're seeing more of them, all the time,
from back East. Feels like they are
fixin' to take over. It's like a disease or
a Plague. A plague of locusts that is.
They think maybe wearing some Sears
and Roebuck jeans, Western style shirt
and leather boots don't so much as have
a crack in them, they'll blend in.
Even they know better than to wear a
string tie. If they had any pride, they'd take
them jeans out and drag 'em behind
the pickup for a few hundred miles,
then wash 'em 'til the color fades to
a natural washed out blue. That is if
they had a pickup. More than likely they
have one of them SUV's. Shoot, no cowboy
I ever knew would get caught dead in one
of them. Where would the gun rack go?
Bet he don't know what a gun rack is,
much less how to shoot one.
Can't carry on a decent conversation
with one of 'em either. You say, "Back in
the day, Ole Barry would have known
what to do." And they look dumber than
usual and ask, "Who's Barry?" And you say,
"Goldwater." And they think you're on about
some new liquid refreshment comes in a
plastic bottle they haven't heard of yet but are
dying to try. That's like going to Louisiana
and not knowing who Huey Long was.
What good are they? Back when I was in
the Rangers over there in The Nam we used
guys like them for target practice.
Guess we missed a few.

Ride Him, Cowboy

"Rustling, we used to call it.
Saturday nights, when the need arose,
we'd stock up on whatever-was-on-
sale-beer, two, three cases Lone Star,
Dixie, PBR, we didn't care. Slam them
down, maybe grab a fifth or two of 10 High,
to make things nice and interesting,
then we'd load up the pickup with gear,
not that we needed much. Hell, the gun rack
is like always stocked anyway, locked and
loaded the way weapons should be,
a couple of lengths of rope, some chains,
lots of Ted Nugent for the stereo, maybe some
gasoline. Hell, what else would you need?
A cattle prod, maybe…then we'd head out
to some fag joint and rope us a few.
Suckers never saw it coming, never knew
what hit them. Not at first anyway. Not until
some of those peckerwoods got into body building.
Know what I mean? Big bodies, little weenies.
Some of those boys actually represented
a challenge. Nothing we couldn't handle,
mind you. Not until we roped us a real live one.
He was slick, I'll give him that. Played it cool.
One of the boys wanted to rope him to the bumper
like usual, let up a little on the bonds and
doesn't that sucker let out with some ungodly
yell and kicked our man right into the next world.
Had a couple of guys laid right out before anyone
knew what happened. Had to put him down without
the usual preliminaries. Spoiled that night's fun.
Fact is, no one much wants to rustle anymore.
Say it's just not the same. Hell, I say, what is?"

Exodus

They acted as if they were twelve
apostles, seven days dead, dancing in
slow motion to scratched platters played
a few rpms below regular speed in some
third world, off road, pickup bar.
Old time black and white movies flashed
on their bodies making everyone seem
more unreal than they already were,
gyrating in some kind of post-dress-
rehearsal-for-a-death, rag.
The one who fancied himself a Technicolor
Judas wore a stained by goat's blood Joseph
coat, led the way into unisex bathroom
for crank and dissolute sex with bony,
washed-completely-out, bleached blonde,
kohl eyed, Botox lipped Madonnas of
the meth lab, an act so difficult to follow
none of the others dared to follow where
their leader had tread. All of them so whacked,
bouncers had to forestall leave taking to
insure the all-important settling of the tab.
All that remained of their swag, held by self-
proclaimed Judas, was a handful of coins
scattered on the bar, insufficient funds to
prevent the kind of beating no man was meant
to endure. If there was a state of being
such as worse than dead, one of the faithful
said, their Judas priest embodied it.
No funeral services have been arranged.

Sympathy for the Devil

After an extended childhood spent
watching MTV stoned on whatever
he could score, he had the alt-rock
look down: Doom Cult t-shirt,
sleeveless and soiled, washed from
black to almost gray, beyond tight
dragged out jeans, pointed shit kicker
boots, all the facial hair he could grow
beneath requisite medusa knot locks.
Told all the slumming, punked out,
dive bar queens, pretenders to thrones
of tough and hard, he was the lead
singer in some heavy metal bar band
that was about to make a quantum leap
into the big time. Were tuning up for
mega gigs once the studio album was
cut and released. In real life he was a
wannabe roadie known for his skill
at rolling perfect doobies and not
much else. Even terminal losers have
a skill. Kept him vaguely employed,
made him known in all the fringe places
make believe rock stars hung out waiting
to overdoses, a moral's charge, or a major
drug bust. Getting lucky, for him, was
a hit of not bad acid, some clean Poontang,
and someone else's demo tape he could
pass off as his own. Had visions of dying,
hitting perfect chords on a wired guitar,
short circuiting waves of electricity instead
of veins, his hair on fire.

Home of the Brave

"Que es mas macho?"
—Laurie Anderson

Murder tourists wearing "America First",
red ball caps, three cheers for the home team
and no one else,
strapped on weapons: from buck knives
to Glock nines, kill or be killed viewpoints,
might be better off dead.
"Make mine a Budweiser-drink American"
either oblivious to, or ignorant of, Belgian
corporate takeover of former All American
brand,
"Speak English as God intended or be gone",
"If God had meant for us to speak other
languages he would have dictated His Word
in another tongue",
anarchist patriots, "Don't Tread on Me" pennants,
flags, decals, tattoos, proclaim, "in the land of
the free, citizens do not have to obey laws
they don't agree with", band together in gangs,
follow their chosen paths directly into
In God We Trust labeled courts, max security
prisons, unclaimed bodies gravesites.
third generation drug abused children, faulty
genes rewired into something barely human,
nearly dead in their teens; even the Marines
can't make men of them.
Predicate felons with rap sheets instead of bios,
parole violation headaches and ulcers, pedal
to the metal Venus overdrive dreams, always
two quarts less than a gusher, a false alarm
away from a fire.

Cries and Whispers/Night and Fog

Maybe this nightmare was actually a
dream, instead of a documentary movie in
progress. All these low flying helicopters
just above the tree line, spaced roughly
a minute apart, search lights spanning
the ground, the back yards, the copses of
trees, flying out over the park, then back
through the neighborhood, back into the gut
of the city where all the action was coming down.
Waking into this odd dream noise felt the way
Captain Willard did, seeing war scenes in the
jungle of his mind, mistaking the overhead
wooden blade ceiling fan for chopper blades
and realizing, with a shock, that he wasn't,
physically in the jungle, but still in Saigon.
But we weren't in Vietnam but in upstate,
New York in some highly choreographed
street drama in progress, the purpose of which
remained a mystery but could only be one thing:
a multi-departmental police raid on drug trafficking
rings and local gangs with national affiliations.
Sirens now, in addition to the copter noise,
bullhorns too, indistinct speeches that could
only be commands, spinning police car lights,
blue and red strobes staining the tree leaves,
the close-together-houses unnatural colors,
even the shadows alive with a kind of fire
and now there is no hope for sleep, and we wonder,
where will they land and what will happen next?
And once awake, will sleep ever be the same again?

L. A. Confidential

All the stories are the same:
sordid and vile, something
that could have been found in an
Xtra Xtra Read All About It rag.
An L.A. Confidential with leaders
like: Leading Man Caught Naked in
Swimming Pool, sub-header revealing:
with rent boys, low end losers, hep cats
with drug habits, bennies and greenies
in cut glass candy dishes for all to partake of,
to insure all night stamina and a special
glow. Blonde Bombshell Seen with Blaxican
House Boy, nothing like a half-breed for
righteous ire, for greasing the poll and
keeping the trim around the garden neat
and well-tended. Every Laurel Canyon
mansion a possible location shot for your
own personal valley of the dolls. Beneath
palm trees, behind every glow light,
pinheads instead of pinups, pockmarked
fetish porn superstars one operation short
of becoming a quad.

Blind date girl about town with Blue Dahlia
lipstick and mismatched ensemble an unsolved
mystery with True Confession cops on scene
commenting, "Did you see the rack on that broad?
What a waste." The powers that be, sleazy
beyond compare. Corruption has a call box,
an area code, and address, a precinct number.
even the innocent guilty.

Inland Empire

Line dancing was never supposed to be
like this: Frederick's of Hollywood
hookers chorus lining, performing a kind
of Texas Two Step to Little Eva's, "Locomotion".
The only train you could imagine them
involved in was group sex with PCP and
lights, camera, action. The whole messed up
scene like an alternate reality, parallel world,
a schizophrenic screen actress's last lucid
moments before the fugue state that shuts
her down. Everyone time tripping like a
Slaughterhouse Five, like a midnight
ride down Mulholland Drive that
never ends. Even she isn't sure what is
real and what is not except where all
the homies and hookers converge on a corner
of Horse Latitudes and Tropic of Cancer,
a place in their minds near where the concrete
rivers overflow, spilling gasoline fed fires like
rainbows over the pavement, the gathered faces
unearthly like alien beings never before seen
anywhere but up on the big screen, larger than life,
larger than the sky where all the stars are,
exploding like supernova roman candles,
one after the other, until nothing is remains
but stardust memories and this.

Raging Bull

The first time I saw
a man beaten so badly
he might die was Live
on TV in a ring

Benny "Kid" Paret,
gloves down, arms limp,
eyes closed. Emile Griffith
punching away, relentless,
the ref right there, watching,
transfixed.

Why doesn't he stop it?
The man is out on his feet.
Stop it now.
Why?

Some called it a grudge match.
At the weigh in you should never
pat your opponent on the butt,
whisper in his ear, "Maricon,"
even if it was true.
Benny did that.

It wasn't "Raging Bull,"
the movie, it was Friday Night
at the Fights.

Speedy Alka Seltzer
Bob and Ray as Bert and Harry Piels
Gillette Foamy
and their razor blades

Blood on the canvas.
The ref raises Griffith's hand,
announces the winner.

There must have been a bell
ending the round,
not that it was necessary.

No sound at all except Benny's
handlers lying on the mat next to him,
trying to get him to speak,
waving smelling salts under his nose,
to no avail.

Doctor in the ring, a stretcher,
the limp body hoisted
from the canvas, everyone else
looking down, watching, even Griffith.
It's not easy to kill a man.

In a title match
On National TV
Then defend the belt.

Friday nights have never been
the same since.

2-American Psycho

American Psycho

"Want to know what God thinks of money?
Look at who he gave it to."
                                    —Dorothy Parker

Back in the day, he was known on
campus as The Pharmacist.
Made a small fortune selling bad acid,
ingestibles cut with rat poison,
stink weed pot cut with strychnine.
Ran for student council and got his ass
kicked, despite all the party favors
he handed out at keggers, frat mixers,
school sponsored concerts: no one forget
a bad dope deal and everyone was on
drugs, or pretending to be. Later claimed
he won the election, that he was at Woodstock
sharing blow with Jimi backstage and
some So Co from a pint with Janis though
he was maybe nine at the time and thought
Woodstock was in Vermont. Parlayed
his drug money into extra-legal activities
on sure bet schemes like gun running into
Central America under the guise of Import-
Export business trading durable goods
and food stuff using contacts he made with
the feds ratting out his drug suppliers and
selling out his partners in various underground
enterprises, selling them out to the highest bidders
no matter what kind of interests they claimed to
represent. Liked zaftig women who could have
worked as live Reubens nude models in another
life. Liked them waiting on plush pillows like
Prado Naked Maja perpetually ready to be ravished,

no expenses spared, even the extras. Especially
the extras. What's five thousand plus for a weekend
among friends? Occasionally his staff provided
a surprise to go with his call-in service: nubile,
underage Traci Lords body doubles, no one in
their right mind was going to card, as a private
joke in the films they were going to make of these
Close Encounters of the Obscene Kind.
Having something like that in the bank was
better than money. Guys like him were always
going to want to do, let's-make-a-deal to
acquire an endless supply of deep down and
dirty girly action.

The Proposition

The choices presented were not choices
at all: life in a place jesus wouldn't ride
an ass through after 40 days in the wilderness,
or a no-life-support, unarmed, on the run
existence no outlaw in his right mind would accept.
Death was the third option, and though it seemed
like the best one, given the other two, it was an
on the run kind of night. Was like a bad dream
with Nick Cave and the Bad Seeds in it:
all murder ballads and dead maidens in river
shallows, wilting garlands and a rogue lily
clutched to her pale chest, free floating images
like a nightmare with a waking life migraine.
All the days that followed, all the soundtrack music
that played on the road, was an elegy for civilization's
end. Survivors of the great burn either scavenger
or cannibals, or part of an even worse proposition:
living in a desert on the edge of a nowhere Australia
outback: all killers and psychos in training,
robbers and rapists, and the three old men
that watched them all as judge, jury, and hangman
in Cinemascope like the Hateful 8 with dust
storms instead of blizzards. Life a movie where
everyone dies in the end, even the horses they
rode into town on and there was nothing but
bad seeds to sow on fallow ground at highway's
end where road warriors play chicken in
their modified-for-suicide rides, flaming out
where they met, head on, and those few who
remained, warmed their hands on the fiery remains.

Lilith

All the like a rolling stone education
taught her was how to French inhale
menthol cigarettes. How useless all
those Emily Post rules for life and living
were, in the here, and now, and the everywhere else.
That the worm at the bottom of the bottle didn't taste
half as bad as it looked if you drank enough
of what it had been marinated in or smoked
enough Mexican with the bad boys she met,
breaking curfew on weekends or on bogus family
emergency weekend passes that became a kind of
South Texas dirty two nighter in trailer parks
or sleazy dry rot sleepy bye roach motels.
All the money spent on ballroom dancing lessons
were wasted as all she ever did was a down home
dirty boogie to honky tonk blues and garage band
rhythms that ended up as a Cowgirl room horizontal
tango she excelled at and craved like a matching
set of butterfly tattoos. All the cotillions,
formal invitation, coming out as a deb dinners,
didn't prevent her from hooking up with a
hardscrabble, long haired, husky voiced,
steel guitar player, pushing forty with a rap
sheet instead of a pedigree and a serious bad
attitude he substituted for manners.
What she loved about his outlaw life couldn't
be taught in any prep school she'd ever heard of
and what she lived for was the magic his fingers
made on the strings and the dynamite in his
low rider jeans, even loved his, probably made-up
name, Wormwood Scrubs, and how her parents
eyes crossed every time he opened his mouth
and spoke. Everything about him was enough

to induce coronary occlusions in parents, authorities
of any kind, and that was good enough for her.
After all, she was twenty-one, her trust fund
was enabled and she could display the look of
a contented woman who knew she could dress
a hillbilly in a three-piece suit but you
can't make him sing hymns. That, my friends,
she thought, was having the best of two worlds.

Snake Pit

How did it come to this uncontested
divorce from modern life? Was it failing
the white glove test too many times?
Dust on the mantelpiece and on the upper
bookshelves? The dinner hour martinis
that were not properly chilled, that had
too much vermouth, that had the wrong
brand name of vermouth? Not enough
enthusiasm for weekly book club/coffee
klatch, discussing latest Harold Robbins,
Jackie Suzanne, Margaret Mitchell...?
That, "You know something is happening
but you don't know what it is" afternoons,
not paying proper attention during contract
bridge, bidding five no trump when the call
was for spades? The heedless losing of the
rubber, the game, the hands that followed?
Ignoring the advice of golf pros, skipping
sessions with tennis instructors for drawing
classes, drinking black coffee instead of tea?
Being labeled a woman on the verge of a
nervous breakdown, prescribed sleeping
pills, mother's little helpers, you can't wake up
from or fully function after, in half-coma state,
logy and confused? A voluntary confinement/
rest cure would cure what ails. As if consorting
with neurasthenics, obsessive rockers in place,
chronic pacers, howlers, hand wringers, talking
to shadows people, would be restorative,
as if it would do anything but drive a person
mad. A few weeks of this and she fits right in.

The Family

The family were all jesus junkies
spouting Old Testament verses from
Genesis all the way to Exorcist.
Thought thy road and thy staff that
comforted you was for inflicting
GBH, grievous bodily harm, on
sinners and miscreants most of whom
were blood relatives from the legal
woman or ones from a previous existence
before he heard the word and followed
the dark path to where he was now.
Thought women's liberation was
the freedom to have more children,
create disciples for the cause whatever
it might be this week or for picket
lines at funerals for soldiers killed
in service of their country, a duty
they saw as doing the devil's work.
His sermons were all fire and brimstone
and those who followed him lived in
thrall like debtors in a prison that
they could never escape from.
Convinced he would never die,
that he was the living embodiment of
our lord god, father of all things,
he refused to recognize Death when
he saw him in the mirror but Death
recognized him.

Last Rights: The Singers

When they were kids, all their time
not spent before mirrors making
themselves look half-dead with
black eyeliner, Kohl highlighting
and maroon lipstick, was spent
discovering the pleasures of super-
market dairy aisles: Whip-its followed
by select pharmaceuticals: Nyquil
and 24-Hour brain suppressors and
the boys who obtained it for them.
Then the airplane glue huffed in brown
lunch bags but who had no energy
for anything like sex after.
Glueys had their place in life but
bed was not it. Which was basically,
okay, all that writhing and groping,
followed by the ritual exchanging of
body fluids, was both disgusting and
distracting from their main purpose
in life: following their dream to become
lead singers in a grunge band.
Finding actual musicians, who dressed
like Salvation Army rejects, smelled
like dumpster diving champions of
the world, and couldn't carry a tune
if their lives depended on it, was no
problem at all. All they had to do
was hang in clubs where the word
"dive bar" was invented, ones that
thought constant fit inducing, flashing
neon lights, passed for atmosphere,
had no windows or AC, and a john

with no doors, that flushed more often
than it didn't, but not by a wide margin.
Sitting at the bar, stoned nearly blind,
dressed like harpies on the make,
totally obvious to everyone and
everything, was a variation on a theme
of Field of Dreams, sit there and they
will come. And, of course, they did.
Choosing the right ones was a process
of elimination: falling down drunk or
zoned completely out on reds, meant
you were out, but speed ballers, yeah
speed ballers were the nuts: all that energy
to spare and the brains of a gerbil on a
treadmill, was in. Not having material
was a bit of a problem solved by obtaining
twin savage god tattoos on their chests,
multi-piercing every visible body part,
and raiding the Good Will store for anything
resembling cut up granny clothes they
could maim further and create a look
and a catchy name for the group
like Last Rights and you were golden.
It was the look that mattered, after all,
the vibe you created on stage, I mean,
Hell, who listens to what anyone actually
screamed into those mikes? Living past
the age of 27 was an issue for most of the
people they'd envisioned becoming as
none of them seem to make it beyond
that point. But 27, Hell, 27 was so far in
the future even thinking about it was

a waste of their valuable time. They would be the singers in a band, they would thrive, they would be the stuff of legend.

Looking for Mr. Goodbar

Most of the bars she spent time in
had signs that said, "Don't Leave
Your Valuables Unattended-
Management Assumes No Liability
For Lost or Stolen Items".
Not that anyone could read, or
would read, a sign that didn't have
discount drink prices listed.
After a couple of trips to the Ladies
she asked one of the older women,
someone who could, maybe, be thirty,
why all the girls brought their drinks
with them to the bathroom?
"Honey, in a place like this one,
the last thing you want to do is leave
a beverage handy so some guy can drop
something in it. Takes all the work
out of scoring for them, but I can assure
you, honey, you don't want to go there.
Waking up on a concrete floor somewhere,
in a puddle of piss, no jeans, panties ripped
to shit, no phone, not a dime for a call
or a cab, gives new meaning to the term,
Wasted. Long necks work for me just fine.
They're nice and portable and, in a pinch,
make a mighty fine weapon."
She thought about the scrum of industrial
strength losers flexing their muscles at
the bar, the easy access to date rape drugs,
and how, for a double sawbuck, you could
convince a bartender to look the other way,

develop hysterical blindness, or do the drop in deed himself. Thought about how she might wake up, if she was lucky, face to face with Mr. Goodbar, a straight razor clenched between his teeth.

Diary of a Mad Housewife

If the truth be known, she took all those,
Visiting Poet/Writer in Residence gigs,
just to get out of the house.
Her old man could have cared less what
she did with her writing as long as she
gave him space for his true passion: making pots
of money designing Brutalist buildings
and screwing all the nubile interns who came to
worship at his drawing board.
Every semester on the road for her, promised
potential new bedmates, as sex with her husband
was as dismal as it was rare, generally a farce
of nature after too much wine, good food, and
occasional recreational drugs.
Of course, they had children, conceived in what
appeared to her now as: forlorn hope disguised
as love, and a deluded optimism for a future neither
one of them believed in.
They had grandchildren, as well, kids she spoke of
often to convey to her listeners that she was
in a committed relationship but she was willing
to be flexible as long as it went no further
than a brief, but memorable, affair.
Maybe there would be a body builder among
the latest acolytes, this occasionally happened,
even established poets worked out, as she did,
every morning to clear her head and flex muscles
she might need later on for more intimate
encounters. A Martial Art expert would be a
refreshing change; the poetry was awful but
the sex was great.
Most of the hopefuls would be women.

There was no avoiding that.
She had tried one or two out for trial runs but
they were unsatisfactory as she just couldn't
swing that way.
All of them shared one trait: unrealistic expectations.
There was no avoiding it and most of her job
entailed letting them down gracefully and with tact.
Hell, you never knew when a great line might sneak
into a dreadful poem, a line she could steal and
pretend was her own.
If someone complained, who were they going to believe:
a neophyte nobody or the visiting writer in residence?

Napalm Sunset

They flew out of Subic Bay,
destination unknown, somewhere hot.
It was always hot wherever they went,
or would be once they got there.
The kind of work they specialized in
wasn't written up in logbooks or
recorded on mission accomplished
sheets. Was so ultra-classified
they weren't classified at all, in fact,
never happened, whether they succeeded
or not. Between them they had more
battle scars than a squad of grunts
halfway through an active tour in
the green. "Death from Above"
was their Proverbs, and "I Believe in God,
God is Napalm", their Psalms.

Back from their highly productive
days in country, torching villes
and disposing of the remains,
they were every bar girl's fantasy
in faded khakis: horny, well-heeled,
silent men with wads of American and
a taste for the unusual, regardless of the cost.
A few days of cheap thrills and they would
be thoroughly sated, ready to rock n roll,
to saddle up and ride into a napalm sunset.

Walk on the Wild Side (2)

"Willner tells me that his friend Lou Reed
clung hungrily to life, hungrily, but then
calmly took his leave." Nick Cave

It's not a jazz suite they hear cruising
mean streets, but a grand piano,
Van Cliburn assaulting a Russian composer
with deft, lean fingers, a pale ghost
with a spray of strawberry blonde hair.
Such nice, erect posture for a man!

Champagne cocktails in dim lighted
loge seats, Upside Down Manhattans
and Dirty Martinis in wide mouthed
glasses: the sun never sets inside these
crystal glass filled unlicensed bars.
The sun never rises either.

But the men who lurk outside, French
lipping hand rolled cigarettes know what
goes on inside, hone brass knuckles
to points, carry a lead weighted cosh
for sandbagging the unwary who stumble
into their paths. They aren't the type who
will complain about a simple assault,
a robbery involving goods and services.

On Christopher Street and well beyond,
those in the know are hip to where the
soft parade is headed. Warn against sleeping
with angels, drunk and in the raw, on a Fire
Island public beach. Those who dare, suffer
the consequences. This is what life is when
you choose walking the wild side.

The Spy Who Came in From the Cold

In the dream, there was fireworks.
Not tracer rounds, contrails fouling
the sky, not incoming rounds, shells
that exploded in no man's land you
wouldn't hear until it was too late
to react. There was barbed wire in
those days and nights, strung between
deeply embedded poles impeding
progress on foot in knee deep mud.
There were fox holes, bomb craters,
hand dug trenches filling with water,
scum of gasoline on top, dead things
floating inside. Maimed and disfigured
things, formerly living things bloating
now, unrecognizable. Letters home
in strapped leather pouch, poems written
on torn envelopes, snap image photos.
all scraps of nothing now, blood spotted,
singed. Also, among the missing, hand
drawn maps, pages of numbers of no
discernible pattern, codes, maybe,
secrets that will never be revealed.
The hand that held them all, severed
at the wrist, illuminated from above
by star bursts of color fading to black.
A staggering man heads toward a
temporary HQ bunker. Has something
to say but there is no one there to listen.
Silent fireworks explode, poison gas seeps,
a low cloud of it descending with dead embers
from above, all of it falling with the sky.

The Waitress

Men in suits imagine themselves posing
for cover of Black Belt magazine: white
shirts open, black chest hair turning gray,
exposed, gold neck bling, a single edged
razor blade affixed to a chain. Sit at a four
top table. Order elaborate cocktails with
precise instructions. Blood red steaks,
so rare the cow might moo when they cut
the outer, blackened flesh. Want everything
pronto. Yesterday, if possible. Call their
server: Honey, Dear, Babe . . .
Say, "Be a good girl and follow orders.
We tip big because we're large men."
She can hear them thinking, what they imply,
"You know what we mean by Big."

Makes sure their drink order is exactly right.
Says she'll be right back with their food.
Feels their eyes on her as she walks away.
Brings them death warmed over on a plate
and drops the food, not quite sliding it into
their laps. Waits.

Waits for the inevitable reaction, "What's this?"
"Your food."
"It's not what we ordered."
"No shit, Sherlock."
"We're not going to eat this. Take it away
and bring us our steaks."
"Take it or leave it. That's the only meal
you're getting from me."
"We want to speak with the manager. Now!"
"You'll have to make do with me.

As the owner, I'll speak for her. She couldn't
make her shift today and I'm filling in."
"You're being exceedingly rude to paying
customers."
"You've obviously mistaken me for someone
who gives a shit."
They stare.
She waits.

Jaws

They called themselves Great White,
suggesting what? The man eating
shark from the movie that terrorized
swimmers for a generation, a movie that
took place not far up the coast from where
they were playing, in Warwick at
The Station. Maybe someone thought
they were The Who, staging an outdoor pyro
show, inside. One that featured stuff that
ignited the ceiling, the walls stuffed
with sound insulating foam, producing
black smoke and flames long before the first
song was through. Boys in the band must
have thought, "Holy Shit", were among the
first to boogie out backstage door, blocked
behind them by a bouncer who insisted this door
was for band use only, while many of the onlookers
stood transfixed, stoned, or just plain slow to react.
Headed for the door they came in, once the lights
went out, power failed, hundreds headed to
the same small space, a table in the way,
so much confusion, and panic just a stampede away.
A hundred dead, burned, trampled, suffocated,
even a member of the band who escaped,
but unwisely, went back inside to save his ax.

All those not coded bars, grandfathered in or
never inspected, in basements with sunken sub-floors
for dancing and only one narrow way in or out,
not even a small window to break.

Or all those makeshift second floor spaces in
warehouses accessed by a ladder, windows
too high to jump from, alleyways strewn with
garbage, wooden structures no one ever used,
tinder and fuel, no sprinklers inside, no extinguishers,
nothing but stuff that burned. Too many heads to count,
capacity never determined, not that anyone followed
an occupancy suggestion. How many were
spaced on party drugs? hallucinating and drinking
industrial strength cocktails to mellow the groove?
Details matter when people die in places aptly named
Ghost Ship Collective.

And after the burning is done, the ax and the blade
and the jaws of death, that are the instruments that finalized:
just another successful experiment in terror. "It all happened
so fast." Survivors say. A foot per second according to
The Great White fire re-creation. Details matter
when you can't breathe, when fire bites your ass.

Patriot Games

They must be brothers: of the grape and
of the flesh. Drinking Screwdriver Cocktails
in a can, the concept that changed the face
of alcoholics at bus stops everywhere.
Are the voices in cell phones on board,
relaying day's adventures getting rousted
both in Schenectady and Albany, the far reaches
of bus plus route. Say they are headed for Colonie,
dead center between the two, begin acting out
after last stop before theirs, once bus shifts
into passing lane to make time, start chanting
how they are, "Proud to be Americans.
Hope their man Trump does a number on all
the rag heads. Now that he's got the bombs
they'll get fried for sure. Build a wall.
Yeah, go for it, Trump! He's the man all proud
Americans love. Proud Americans! Proud Americans!
That's us. Suck on this you Hillary lovers.
You know she killed people?" Don't elaborate
on just who that was just so proud to be
Americans, "textbooks cases of why no one
in their right mind voted for him," a black guy
says once they are outside. "That's what
patriotism looks like now", an old guy says:
Two drunk guys in mid-afternoon, crossing
a four-lane highway against the light, giving
the world the finger.

Murder, My Sweet

They called themselves freelancers,
stringers for some murder tourist rag
that imagined human suffering and
atrocity exhibitions were the last pure
sensations left to man. Preferably
copiously illustrated in lurid colors,
the more graphic the better.
Have passports stamped at every hot spot
on the planet as if they were hop scotching
to every danger zone in a race against time
to see who could rack up the most frequent
flyer miles, to the most inhospitable places.
A few weeks in a remote outback, or
a jungle wattle and daub hut, and they
would be willing to sell their souls for
an eight pack of pre-made Slippery Nipple
shooters. Consorted with all the local gangsters,
professional killer, and pallbearers, free
basing coke and, whatever else was on the
menu, in an attempt to blend in. Reported on
places so bleak, in a style so whacked out
it was almost impossible to read, but on they
went and their assignments tripled. Ended up
somewhere the whores all had black roots
growing out as all the peroxide had gone to
treating the wounded, and there were always
more wounded than any makeshift clinic
could handle.
Said sex under fire was the hottest ever.
Nothing was a bigger turn on than imminent
death, assuming they would cruise through
unscathed, just as they had everywhere else.
Amazing how wrong a person could be about
a simple thing like that.

Portrait of a Lady

Everything about her screamed: disgraced
aristocrat, all of the airs but none of the money.
Had Moet tastes on a Cold Duck budget,
claiming to like all the best things in life
from Bach to Beethoven and beyond.
Said, "You know that piece Bach wrote
for his insomniac patron? The one where
the guy is so into playing he was humming
along on a live recording and played so well,
they released the album anyway. The ones
not scandalized by the sacrilege thought it
was the greatest record ever and it sold like
crazy. You could buy it today if you wanted to."

Somehow, you just knew she only referenced Bach,
as she was overly familiar with fugues, not the
kinds he wrote, but the ones you experienced
after a three-day binge on white powder and
tequila azul, stuff she copped from two Mexican
mules willing to share on a run they ended up
two kilos light of a full load.

Having survived the civil wars between two states
of mind, she seemed to think everyone she met
should kneel down and kiss those gold-plated rings
she wore, ones that were trying to pass themselves
off as the real thing. Dressed in consignment shop robes,
looking as if she was a few IQ points north of brain
dead, following her last vision quest dream where
she was a hand maiden to one of the three Christs
of Ypsilanti, a vision like a caustic solution that
melts all the silk fabrics of her mind.

Murder on the Orient Express

Maybe he thought adding bulk
to his body meant an increase in
brain power as well. That if he
channeled Peter Ustinov and Albert
Finney, he could solve crimes like
a Murder on the Orient Express.
Failing that, he assumed everyone
was guilty of something and if he
had all the suspects shot then the problem
of where the dead body on the train
came from, who put it there, and why,
would just disappear until the next train
to the East, where the same MO occurred
suggesting a serial killer was still
on board. Killing everyone would
solve the problem, eventually,
ten million dead enemies of Stalin
can't be wrong. It felt like an
advertising slogan for a puppet
state when it was said but it wasn't.

Death Becomes Her

She came from a place no one
had a name for. Anyone who had
been there never questioned Death Becomes Her
why you would leave as, once someone
was gone, they never came back.
Even the stop lights were lonely
on what passed for main street
having nothing to stop and go for.

She said that she had never dreamed
as where she was born is where
imagination went to die of hunger
and neglect, even the bones of images
became brittle and dry there like dust
that had no real substance to it.

Her old man had been blind and useless,
reduced to a drooling stammer that
passed for need and want. Was incontinent
and thirsty for beer he could only
drink through a straw, hands shaking
so bad from the need of it; he could not
hold what he had to have. She never
had a mother.

Waited years to hitchhike out as there
was never anyone passing through or
leaving once the Interstate came through
fifty miles South in another world that had
actual people in it. Figured the only way
out otherwise was flat on her back or
feet first dead and it made no difference
to her which as long as it was somewhere else.

Once way out of town she set up shop
in sleazebag roadhouse along some two
lane straightway to Hell Michigan and places
beyond. Forty bucks American and she'd show
you a real good time. Well, something different
anyway. There is no accounting for what men like
in a woman or how they will express it.
If indifference moved you, she was a woman
for the ages. Death becomes her.

After the Rehearsal

He auditioned all the boys
and girls, personal, in his office,
one on one.
Spread the rumor that if his casting
couch had kept a diary it would
have made Casanova blush.
Would have revealed detailed
information The Hite Report,
Kinsey and Masters and Johnson
had missed.
Claimed all the behind the scenes
work had made him old before
his time, and that might have been true,
in a way, if all the communicable
diseases he had caught and the immunity
to the miracle drugs that were required
to cure them, counted as adding rings
to the tree.
Said he had an eye for talent and
a gift for nurturing it, with a straight
face, when everyone knew it was more
of a, "You do something for me and I'll
do something for you," kind of arrangement.
Liked to proclaim that his work was
essentially thankless, foreswearing
personal gain and glory, while compiling
the kind of portfolio that made Wall
Street players envious.
"It was all about the Art, the theater
and the people that made it happen,"
was his standard interview line that
meant, "As long as it benefits me
in the long run."

Might even have convinced himself that
all the lies he told were the truth,
which it may have been, in a way,
the way good propaganda has an element
of reality, the way self-congratulation may
be seen as modesty, to the recipient, but
seen as a mockery of the truth by everyone else.

Drug Store Cowboy

"It's not the bullet that kills you-it's the hole"
—Laurie Anderson

The journey home is like a vision
quest variation: instead of finding
the alchemical key to transmuting
lead into gold or the answer to the
question of what life is? but a journey
to the West, seeking the perfect
combination of chemicals and alcohol,
the one that would explode parameters
of being and seeing into a new dimension
of altered realities and sartorial bliss.
The record of his sampling the new,
the untested, and the arcane is a mixture
of film clips, spoken word, and dream
diaries collated under a working title:
My Own Personal Yage Letters.
He is like Burroughs writing to Allen
from the wild, only in a more civilized,
American sort of way, a William Least
Heat Moon with a designated
limo driver and air conditioning.
Still, he was dedicated and willing to go
anywhere sources, even unreliable ones,
especially the unreliable ones, suggested.
Finally made his appointment in Samarra
with a black messiah/ known junky priest,
in a bar called The Hole in the Wall known
for an infinity of back bar mirrors: no matter
where you were or what you did, there was clear
view of yourself both coming and going.

Sitting there is a perfect Chimes at Midnight
moment: a girl, a gun and a pissed off party
of the third kind. Even the bartender is
armed. Wears a white face mask to conceal
who he might be, dispenses death in a beaker
like nitro with a lime, you are expected to
drink, no questions asked. Or failing that,
take this blotter acid with and lemon and salt
chaser after drinking something from a bottle
holding a diet of worms. Given the choice,
that is not a choice at all, ingest the pill that
takes you there and brings you back,
if you're lucky. Heed the advice:
"When the guns go off, better duck.
This is not a test. This is not a race."

The Hunger

"What do you do?" She asks.
"I take pictures of dead people."
—Nick Seeley, *Cambodian Noir*

It must have been the correct answer.
She says, "Psychedelic Furs make me
feel warm all over like Ketamine and
Coke." Leans in close, French inhaling
some local loco weed like it was a
mentholated Kool long, eyes like laser
pointer lights on mine.
"I'm more of an Insane Clown Posse
kind of guy. Anarchist rapping to the
apocalypse. Just a Juggalo, everywhere I go..."
"Want to go someplace more private?
I know all the secrets of The Ages.
The ones I don't know, I'll make up
as we go along."
"Sounds great to me. What's the catch?"
"Just keep an open mind." She says,
seductively smiling, "Let me write
the instructions to my place for you."
I watch her write, hand the paper to me
and turn. See her long legs disappear
into as denim mini-skirt, tank top tight
and inviting. Shoulder length black hair
sweeping across her shoulders as she walks.
Everything about her says sex and death
and not much in between.
The written instructions to her place
are simple: Follow the long, narrow
two lanes until you arrive nowhere.
Turn left and keep driving until you
can't go on.

It would be a place so remote even
vandals, door to door rip off experts,
and Murphy artists wouldn't go.
It would have a five-stool counter diner
no one ever went to with daily breakfast
specials with names like: Death Warmed
Over and you would order one just to see
what it would look like. It might not be
the last thing you ever did but
awfully damned close.

The Professionals

Booked banquets like casting calls for
Chorus girls, grade B scream queen actresses:
if the feedback was good, you moved
from sales conventions to nominating
committees, top drawer political rallies
with state senators, congressmen,
governors with bodyguards always nearby.
Sometimes, after the show was over,
there were call backs, secluded nights way
out of town in suites wired for video and
sound. Not that home movies were part
of the original contract: what they didn't
know, won't hurt them, unless blackmail
was involved. After all this was America
and you could get whatever you wanted,
if you paid for it. Maybe even health care.
Certainly, no questions asked, no fuss,
no muss, assignations. Sometimes the tips
would blow your mind, as long as your looks
lasted and your body held up. There are no
401k's, no pension plans for bad habits
acquired on the job, no STD riders on non-
existent universal health care packages,
no actor's guild rest homes waiting when
the funds ran out, when the jobs offers stopped.
Only less and less attractive dives to run
client searches, longer nights downing cocktails,
and whatever else was on offer. After a while
even alcohol can't erase what mornings bring.

All that's left memories of state dinners with
false prophets dressed in cummerbunds and
tails, wearing low cut dresses with just enough
bad taste to inspire a strange feeling of
tenderness and lust, a smoker's cough and
agents that won't take your calls.

Naked Lunch

Manual typewriter left over from
a Naked Lunch dream sequence
scene.
Fingers like beaks of oversized
Bosch birds pecking at keys
covered in flesh that bleeds each
time the surface tension is breeched.
Random wordplay poems that are
alive, syncopated as rain on a hot
metal roof or automatic weapon shells
expelled after lock and load fire.
Two days without a drink and
the paid-by-the-week room stinks
of garbage, even the sink, the tub
overflowing; cigar stubs burning.
It's always four in the morning
somewhere when there is nothing
to drink.
Every day and night the same,
even the walls crawling with dream
creatures, insects and the exterminator
is coming with his magic powders,
the fairy dust, that cures the shakes,
kills bugs dead, what passes for life
here.
Burroughs called the new state of mind,
being, The Interzone, but it is much
worse than that, than a place where time
and space have no meaning.
This is Death Valley at high noon,
even the cats in heat.
Everyone smokes in hell.

Big City, Bright Lights

Lying in bed in the no air,
open window night, lit by
five alarm empty warehouse
fire two blocks away but feels
as if it were in another life,
somewhere else.
As the floodlights crisscross
the fully involved, brick faced
building, asbestos dust falls
with specks of roofing, debris
wafted by westerly winds,
poison flakes falling like out-of-
season snow, or a twister unleashed
by a mad god intent on punishing
his unholy children for a litany if
unnamable sins. Lying, inert,
paralyzed by alcohol ennui,
a general lack of interest in a life
that began in pain and ends in
sorrow. Four empty pints and one
to go, balanced on a lead paint window
sill, white once, but something else
now. Listening to a silent fugue
for a heart sick soul and radio that
always plays a pavane for a dead
princess. Blank faces and empty
minds on every floor above and below.
The fire burns.

Born on the Fourth of July

He was the kind of guy who bragged
about his near-suicidal exploits:
playing chicken with commuter trains
for spending money and weed.
If there was danger involved or a dare,
if it was something you could only lose once,
he was on it and had all the near miss
scars to prove it. Saw the "Deer Hunter"
and decided he wanted to be like
the Christopher Walken character when
he grew up: earn a ton of money and
go out in a head capping, blood splatter
of glory. Managed the Walken look
but none of the skills or the money.
Had one too many close encounters
with a few tons of moving metal and was
reduced to earning his folding money
racing motorized wheelchairs over
uneven sidewalks or cars through
intersections against the turning light.
Customized his wheels with glitter
and day glo pennants, racing stripes
and multi-colored ostrich feathers.
Honed his technique after years of
practice but could not account for what
he couldn't see: a car turning a hard,
not-bothering-to-slow-to-a-full-stop,
right on red around a parked Hummer
and an SUV. Didn't matter that he was
well within the painted yellow crosswalk,
lines. Exercise Caution and No Right Turn
on red signs are only as useful as the
inclination to read them and follow directions.

The Trip

Parties that begin on Fridays
and end on Sunday afternoons.
Parties that conclude only when
the mole people arise from their
watery graves to don dark glasses
against the sun. Party goers who
are not so much drunk as disembodied.
all their gray matter dissolved,
body moving by rote. Time for
all the hung-over party people
acquires a new meaning, feels as
endless and as empty as when two
black holes collide in deep space.
None of the party people speak as
they crawl about the new, too well
lighted world. How could they?
Afflicted as they are by space brain,
a form of alcohol induced dementia
characterized by dead central nerve
centers, frozen vocal cords, swollen
tongues. Oh, the haze of all those
parties. The ones that cut your heart out
and replace them with vital pieces left out
and the ones where the weak are primed
by stomach pumps and the strong survive
to drink again. Some are fascinated
by parties, others appalled, but none
were bored or said they wouldn't come
back for more.

Angels and Insects

After decades of late-night commuting
home by bus every law broken is little
more than another page from an
on-the-road-show version of a Divine
Comedy: The Central Avenue Canto.
On display: drunks with knives
knocked senseless into seats by bus
acceleration, more in a coma than a
deep restful sleep, pre-teens admiring
older brother's handguns they are
underage transporters for,
initiation rites into gangs already assured.
Ten-dollar crack whores making a deal
for a cheap trick or a bindle, roll your
own doobie brothers in back of the bus
with the stacked deck, high stakes,
card players, of no-luck-involved games,
stench women and men in disabled
seating, so rank, a voluntary: "clear the
area rule", is in effect despite standing room
only crowd. And the garden variety seat
rockers, idiot savant timetable sayers,
the end-is-near prophets, rummies sipping
sprits from dark plastic water bottles
with a flexible straw. And the pick pockets,
sneak thieves, backpack stealers, cut purses
one and all, but a certifiable death and a live
all-the-way sex act the only exceptions to
the rule until the new age of electronics
that finds a woman traveler trapped in
the middle of nowhere between stops

sitting by a large, unkempt man with a
tablet streaming hard core porn, sound on
high, resolution clear . . . what are her options?
What is the protocol? How does she escape?

The Black Book

"I met distantly related survivors, frail and remote,
grave as ghosts. One showed me a cross she kept
in her purse for when the Nazis came back."
—Howard Kogan, "In the End"

In the end, where the dead live,
all the clock's hands have melted
and turned into icy blades of
frozen glass that reflects the dark
that emanates from moons that rise
in the West and set in the East.
Time has no meaning when all
the clocks have stopped, traffic is
just the way bodies collide when
they walk sightless, as moles, above
ground, tunneling through concrete.
Breathing is a labor when all you
can exhale is methane gas, Zyklon B
and Cyanide. Seeing is limited by all
the residues left behind after heat
lightning has rent all the ozone, making
layers of bodies out of skin and bones.
In the end, a clock without hands is
like the cross at the head of a grave
that holds no body.

3-Exterminating Angels

Badlands (2)

Their forefathers had portraits hung
in museums throughout the West.
Not in national galleries but in museums with
Wanted Dead or Alive legends
beneath hastily sketched pictures and
with price tags attached to each one.
Rode with the Daltons on train robberies,
Pony Express take down excursions,
and armed bank jobs.
Were glorified as outlaws when what they
were doing was felonious behavior
of the most grievous sort.
Migrated all the way South, through Mexico
and Latin America, to some lawless place
where cash was king, and no questions
about where it came from were ever asked.
Raised families and thoroughbreds,
becoming feudal masters, lords of the pampas,
brutal as slave owners, landlords with
on the spot justice meted with a whip
and a pistol. All the peons feared the white,
godless, no-heart, devils who invaded their
land and stole what was rightfully theirs.
Actual commission of crimes skipped
whole generations but reappeared once
the established order was overthrown
and the masters were forced to flee Norte
to the states where they acquired better
weapons than they had access to at home.
Weapons they used to liberate assets
from vaults, wherever valuables were
stored, one daring raid at a time.

Eventually earned their place on a wall,
in mug shots, flip files posted on walls
in post offices, touted, for a time, as
America's Most Wanted.

The Girl with the Dragon Tattoo

A few drinks after hours and she thought
that her life was an epic saga, a high-octane
drama, an action movie like "The Girl with
the Dragon Tattoo: The European Version",
that she was the star of. Her life,
before stimulants, was more Asperger's
than toxic avenger, steeped in international
intrigue masquerading as a bisexual madwoman
on tour as the lead singer of all girl Alt band
that made Patti Smith in her prime seem tame.
Whacked on whatever, she tangoed to an inner music
louder than any juke box made by man
or healed by an alien, gyrating like a heat
seeking, spotlight heliotrope, refueling
her body with more kinetic energy
than a lightning strike, so turbo charged
she needed no head lamps to illuminate
where she was headed in the dark.

Look Homeward Angel

From twenty feet away she looked
like a wayward angel, a silent screen
It girl strutting her stuff and proud
of it. Up close and personal, plastic
surgery scars suggested a prototype
for Bride of Frankenstein too ugly
for a screen test or animation.
Had been rode hard and put away
wet, as in a bloody mess, and was
never quite the same after.
Planned on making up for time lost by
returning all the favors she had received
in kind. She wasn't sure how it would
all work out but one thing was certain,
five alarms wouldn't be enough to put
out all the flames.

A Night to Remember

Nights without sleep, staring at
gray-dark of not-quite-night,
not-quite-dawn and it is always
somewhere between two and four
in the morning. That time when
the barely contained rage of wild men
drinking merges with the seriously
deranged and becomes one.
Is that time when the balanced scales
of Fate shift and unintended
contact becomes a retaliatory shove
and the shove back, elicits a head butt,
or a bottle becoming a club and the skirmish
that ensues, goes from minor battle to
all-out war. Those hours of first responders:
fleets of squad cars, uniformed police
with riot control weapons drawn
followed closely by the EMT's
gurneys fully flexed and ready to go.
Those hours when the Black Maria
becomes an oversized hearse or a death
squad conveyance. Once inside,
locked down or not, no one will hear
you scream.
Those hours when the mayhem goes
from somewhat containable, to out
of control; only the spatter patterns
on the bar walls different, the evidence.

Exterminating Angels

Once they had been someone's
little girls, off to college in preppie
clothes and jeans, who were,
by junior year, looking like they'd
been kidnapped by Rastafarians
who braided their waist length hair
into dreds, clothed them all in Marley
t-shirts, no bras allowed, and distressed
jeans so torn, the fabric was more for
preventing complete display of what
was underneath than actual clothing.
All of them acquired eye brow
and nose rings, diamond studs
where the rings weren't, ear piercings
and bad tattoos, lots of them, everywhere.
If the punk band they formed had a
permanent name it would be:
Exterminating Angels and the one
chord they could play would be backed
by a Ziggy Stardust refugee drummer
on speed, a blind keyboardist, and
a sax player who had won an Andre
the Giant lookalike contest.
Their voices, amid all that cacophony,
was an evil shriek that electrified
crowds, leaving them cold as graveyard
crypt art on a foggy night, their black
angel wings enfolding where those
listening were standing, stiff in a drug
induced haze, in damp overhead lit
spotlights, in cellar bars with no windows,
no in-case-of-fire exits, no ventilation,
just a small portion of hell's half acre
to lie down in.

Wise Blood

When she sat down to write
she was torn between channeling
the Whore of Babylon pursuing
a popeyed haircloth messiah,
and the beauty of Miss Emily in
virginal white and a tri-cornered
hat poet from the outer banks of
Brooklyn, toting a gun she planned
to use on real varmints in an
imaginary garden. The written
results were a confusion of tones
so stark they defied description,
sort of a fugue for wind instruments,
broken strings, and a left-hand only
piano soloist. At readings her costumes
free ranged from Mary Magdalene
on-the-make street walker to Lady Gaga
in nude body suit draped in raw cuts
of leaking-blood, raw tenderloins.
Claimed to believe an oft-stated conviction
that there was a New Testament
of suppressed books before Revelation
and she had been appointed to spread
the Living Word. Acted as if she
had seen what Joseph Smith saw
behind a drawn screen: the flaming
text of the Mormon Angels and only she
would know the way. Read from her
translations of Tribulations, Deviations,
and Retributions suggesting there were
more to follow that had not been given
English names yet. She seemed so
convincing, so eloquent, you could
almost believe.

Man from Planet X

His was a drunkard's path from
one crime scene to another.
Was a parable of self-inflicted
catastrophe, petty theft, shake down
jobs and the odd possessions of
forged instruments and illegal
weapons. All of which led to years
of post graduate work, after jail, to
larger finishing schools, with higher
walls, and better security. Places
where professionals passed along
received wisdom, fool-proof plans,
that would prove to be as worthless
as funny money in a loaded dice,
craps game, with Life. All the chances
he took running down bad leads and
worse connections from these inside
sources, hard time mentors, were of
no practical value once he was released
and had to make his way in the real
world. Became so desperate, injections
of a kind of blue ice into his veins
seemed preferable to the kick-down
grab and run jobs he was compelled to
resort to in lieu of making a living
at serious jobs like armed robbery or
capital felony one. Anything that
provided cash for the next score was
acceptable as long as he wasn't caught.
Was so loaded all the time his skin was
changing unnatural colors from paste
wax white to diamond match tip blue.
His fingers froze what they touched.

The Rules of Attraction

Leaning forward on his barstool
he telegraphs his best move.
One so obvious she wasn't sure
if she should duck or counter punch.
Could see that he was an assortment
of all the bad DNA left over after
the good stuff had been handed out,
the mediocre stuff claimed and only
the dregs remained.
Was kind of shocked when he asked
asked her if she'd like to see his rubbings.
"Rubbings, huh? That's a new one."
Thought, maybe, he had conflated
erotic etchings with rubbings, whatever
that meant. He seemed dumb enough
not to know the difference between
Erotica and Eratica.

So, she went thinking, what the hell?
She had taken more self-defense courses
than this guy had high school credits.
Found out rubbings were impressions
taken from headstones in graveyards,
like you actually took paper and rubbed
charcoal or something over the paper
and inscriptions appeared.
Was actually pretty cool and he had
a big collection.
Wasn't even paying much attention
to the fact that she was in his house,
upstairs, where the bed was.

The Sacrifice

"on the third day we ran out of Pampers, and scotch."
—Wendy Mnookin

and couldn't decide which was worse.
Overhead, low flying war planes
rattle the display plates, knock glasses
from counters, dislodge pictures on walls.
Someone suggests hiding in the storm cellar
or under the dining room table far from
window glass but no one moves.
What would be the point?

White noise on the emergency radio station.
It's like that scene in "The Sacrifice" when
the family stop talking, look up to where
the bombers are, all nervous eyes and silenced
voices, trying to pretend an ending is somewhere
else far away. Or it is like that von Trier movie
where the couple is hiding in the reverse Eden
place, a scene flawlessly cobbled together
from shots from Tarkovsky and the darkest
places inside, where impossible weather
unleashes debris like hail, frozen fire instead
of rain, and the furies that follow the escaping
man are revenants from a not-so-distant past.

On a newly wasted, uncontrolled burn plain,
bewildered sheep look up from.
This is how we live now.

Night of the Living Dead

He was the kind of guy
who thought Poontang was
the capital of North Korea
and that Jesus' Son was a
book about a close relative
of the son of God or a DVD
found at a church rummage
sale that could have been
sold as never watched.
Thought the Summer of rolling
blackouts were the end of the world.
Spent the best part of a night
during one of those, crouched
in a corner of his darkened
shotgun shack room with a loaded
weapon waiting for the mobs
of the undead to come.
Sat listening to water from melting
foodstuff in his freezer fill
the drip pan underneath his
dormant fridge unaware that
he was one pitchfork and a few
burning torches short of a mob.
Thought the sun had gone all red
dwarf in his mind while he slept
but it was just the three-way
bulb on high from a standing
lamp shining in his eyes.

The Witches

"Americans believed in money and copulation.
They didn't believe in death anymore…"
—Pete Hamill, A Killing for Christ

She came from the night
like something one toke over
the line, an apparition in high
heels, torn party dress smudged
with oil, grease, dried blood,
stains no one outside of a forensic
lab could put a name to, said,
"I've been drunk for three days:
yesterday, today and tomorrow."
Her eyes were the color of skin
after quicklime ablutions,
hair like something drowned,
revived, then drowned again.
Stood wavering in half-light
of partially drawn shades and
television screens, an empty
glass in one hand, a flask in
the other. Said in a voice like
rasp files in jagged metal edges,
"Have one with me now or
have one with me later."
It wasn't a question.

Lust for Life

After the last arrest, a battery of tests
reveal he has the same IQ as one of
those squiggly things you see writhing
at the bottom of plastic garbage cans
after trash pickups in the summer.
About the only task he is qualified for
would be pub dart catcher for clockwise,
round robin, all-night team competitions,
a specialty not likely to be of much use inside.

Inside, best options available arrived at:
"Should remain heavily sedated at all times,"
leaving him best suited for a nearly immobile
role as real life model for artists whose work
closely resemble that of Francis Bacon.
"Naked Man Drowning Standing Stock Still
in Communal Shower" was the heavily ironic
title that best represented the last moments of
his life. A subtitle added suggests this work
was a study in gray, drained-of-resonance-blue,
jaundice yellow, and gangrenous green.
Was a finalist for the Turner Prize but did not win,
an injustice if there ever was one. Especially
for a man who maintained a mortal fear of water
in any shape, form, or composition.

The Drowning Pool

This is how it begins:
a sedan through underbrush
up against a tree, a steaming
radiator, full moon reflected on
a lake, driver's side door sprung
open, air bag deployed, blood in
the ruts where grass should be

This is how the movie proceeds:
a handheld camera shakily following
path of car downhill as in every horror
movie ever made. Feet cracking dead
sticks as they go. Pant legs scraping
against shrubbery, scattering leaves.
Hands moving obstacles impeding
progress. Rhythmic, labored breathing,
and the sound of a radio not quite tuned
into a station playing what might have
been country and western music in
another life.

The man from the car stumbling toward
the lake. His button-down dress shirt
torn at the shoulder, blood splatters
on once white cloth. Trouser legs
ripped to the knee, to the thigh, soiled
from contact with wet forest floor.
An open head wound free flowing
down unnaturally pale face. Eyes
trying to focus on what lies ahead,
conscious of what follows behind.

This is where the stationery camera
focuses on the moon on the water,
establishing a shot contrasting to what
is about to happen on the shoreline-pursuer
contacting the man from the car.
Thrashing on shore then a splash.
Then another, louder splash and a muffled
voice speaking words that make no sense.
Red bold type letters superimposed on
the once again tranquil scene:
The Drowning Pool. Unrated.
What happens next is up to you.

Legends of the Fall

The family legend suggested she
was conceived in the mud at
Woodstock during a drug fueled,
love-in, any one of several unknown men
could have donated the fatherly fluids for.
Not that she had a family, per se, a mother,
for sure, who was prone to excesses and abuses
and was about as reliable as a crack whore
past her best-if-used-by expiration date.
More than likely, the sex act that produced spawn
was the one that took place on acid,
in a kind of prefab motel room with walls
so thin you could hear the mice breeding
in the neighboring rooms. No wonder
the daughter was a series of acronyms
no one bothered to diagnose, up the chute
at fifteen, and long gone to parts unknown
and presumed dead, not long after she
began to show. Ended up in some place
that was worse than hell, a suburb where
all the plastic, status seeking people,
went to die and once settled there,
even dead, you still had to earn a living.
Her daughter was about as adorable
and adoptable as one of those human science
experiments gone bad in made for second
reels at drive-in movies no one watched
except in between the acts coming up for air
or to light another joint. By her mid-teens
she had a list of priors longer than the veil
of tears track marks on her arms, her brain
a sieve all the dormant, dying cells slipped
through, only leaving behind habits of
a lifetime, a bloodline, that cannot be broken.

Cabaret

Dressing up as a kind of
Sally Bowles did little to
dispel the fact that the only
trait she had in common
with a doomed torch singer,
in a place that resembled Hell
descending, was the pills and
liquor. A few years of seedy
club dates, that felt more like
getting paid peanuts for slumming
than work, she began to resemble
the bloated person at The Oscars
who fit the description of,
"Who is that person trying to
pass herself off as Liza Minnelli?"
The answer, of course, being,
Liza Minnelli, in late decay,
a bad caricature of the winsome
waif she once was. If life was
a Cabaret this is what her life
had become: locked in a sealed
room, a shaker of gin martinis
losing their chill, the poison pills
taken, the gas jets open.

The Stepford Wives

The widows come all dressed in black,
lace veils clinging to the sides of their
faces, hair tied back in buns, faces
powdered white, pale as death.
Their casseroles are overcooked in
Corning Ware baking dishes: from macaroni
and cheese to green beans and tuna fish,
burned breadcrumbs turning black,
straight-into-the garbage or ready to
feed the birds fresh from the ovens.
They travel in groups of five or six,
ringing doorbells at random, burnt
offerings at the ready, never willing to
speak, their eyes say it all in tears,
their lips bloodless and chapped.
Every neighborhood has them though
few admit to their existence, never
advertise for new ones once the older
ones become infirm or die, replacements
simply appear as if summoned by need,
assume the rounds, making their way
from one tree lined street to another,
children clearing paths for them to
proceed, terrified their house might be next.

Another Day in Paradise (2)

If Jesus lived now
his mug shot would be
on the AP wire as the face
of the man who attempted
to throw a live alligator into
a crowded bar in Florida.
He'd have done something
criminal on the tail end of
a three-day binge like driving
a stolen car into a line of
charity bike racers, taking out
bystanders, competitors, and a
utility pole then, undeterred,
backing up for another go around
despite a steaming, leaking radiator,
detached bumpers, and caved in
windshield. Deployed air bags
don't count. His stained t-shirt
would have an AK 47 decal,
a slogan like "My rights doesn't
end where your emotions begin."
In his next life he would be a
Shotgun Judas with a sawed off,
infiltrating a political rally,
church fundraising event, for
the homeless. His chest tattoo of a
screaming eagle with a US flag
decal in its beak is where the
service revolver bullets go.

Ironweed

After all those nights, waking up
on the front lawn, makeup smeared,
a disarray of torn clothing, terminally
tangled hair and bruised body parts....
Sometimes a new lewd tattoo, swollen
lips, backstage t-shirts that said:
World's Number #1 Groupie,
rock 'n roll tested and approved,
underage and under used no more...
Dew like a second, damp layer of skin,
dope rank and alcohol fumed, lying
down where the black ants and the night-
crawlers thrived.
Exiled from parental refuge, her life
became the back seat of some derelict
Ford shared with a Psych Center runaway
barely able to speak, both of them pale
as mimes without the greasepaint,
always dressed in black to better blend in
with the night they scrounged quarters in,
bills, if they were lucky, for warm beers
in dark bars or Dago Red bought from old men
who only spoke the language of Bocce ball
and homemade vino. Sleeping rough
and ready meant windows rolled tight
against intruders whose fingernails
scratched on tempered glass in bad dreams
becoming worse in a season for purple
Ironweeds turning brown with hoar frost,
the thick white blades of grass like dead
fingers rising from the frozen earth,
reaching out for another life.

The Wanderers

Life has become a straight-to-DVD-,
low budget, no future, apocalypse
movie. In the sense that he had
friends, they'd all be dressed in
no lace Timberland boots, navy
blue Dickie's work pants, white
ruffled dress shirts, only buttoned
at the neck, and with long, greasy hair.
The only variant in their attire and
appearance, would be how many
tear drops were tattooed at the corners
of their eyes. Never more than three.
In most states, if you earned four,
you were eligible for the needle.

Boosting cars and mugging drunk
college students leaving open-to-just
before-dawn college bars where
workers, who celebrated "The dawn,
the Goddamned dawn," with hand
rolled spliffs they shared outside
in a black hole, where two corners met,
and the security cameras could not see.
The existence of such a space was a secret
passed along from one generation of
workers to the next like a secret family
patent for a fortune-making elixir or
the location of a forgotten, long-since-
thought-to-be bricked up entrance to
the personal wine cellars of the owners.

Sometimes these two worlds overlapped, co-existed for brief but memorable intersection in time. These confrontations never ended well.

The Doors

"True sailing is dead."

"For the music is your special friend
Dance on fire as it intends
Music is your special friend
Until the end..."
                    —J. Morrison

After hours, outside some forlorn
whiskey bar, some go-go club their
lack of focus suggests one too many
Alabama Slammers for the road,
too many close encounters of the mosh
pit kind, low grade concussions with
a down-the-drain spiral in their eyes.
Their spiked heels and platform shoes
betray them, making walking part of
the impossible dream of their lives.
That dream where they could time
machine transport themselves back
into LA in the Summer of Love
where their only goal in life would
be to gain admittance to whatever
bar The Doors were playing and fuck
The Lizard King senseless. On stage
if necessary: all the unfiltered spot
lights hot and focused, the pot smoke
raw and thick as China white and
plain rot gut neat consumed in the hold
or on the burning deck of a ghost boat
sailing off the charts to nowhere,
moonlight in their eyes, powdered
crystal for brains.

Diva

There were cigarette machines
in those days. Anyone with enough
change to feed the slots and basic
motor skills, could buy their brand
of choice. Yellow teeth and nicotine
lips were a fashion statement like
black fingernail polish and raccoon
circle eyes; a tattoo across her back
uniting shoulder blades with a chain
of words that said, "Better to have
loved and lost than to live with a psycho
forever."
Coffin nails she called whatever soon-
to-be-extinct butt she favored, tapping
them on the bar to pack the leaves tighter
in some Club Fuck where only the hard
core freaks, S&M dykes, and wannabee
punks bought overpriced, watered down,
formerly name brand whiskies, in neon
lit holes where these never-see-the-light
of day losers tried on the lives of other
people, hoping, someday, to find one that fit.
Wherever she was there was bound to be
some one stroke band a couple of hits
of acid from camcorder immortality,
freaking out during a drum solo when
the sticks turned into serpents or their
electric axes turned hostile and attacked.
The last anyone ever saw of them was
a splash of blue and green hair on a neon
background, threatening to spontaneously
combust, dousing themselves, the stage,

and anyone standing nearby, with fire
extinguisher foam before the lights went up
and everyone went blind.

Suddenly, Last Summer

"None of it was ours: The Alleghenies
the fog-strangled mornings of March
cicadas fucking to death on the sidewalks"
—William Brewer

You come from the pits of someplace like
West Virginia: not the coal mines but
the opioid factories, meth lab towns strung
out in a line like strip malls, double wide
and twice as lethal as chemistry experiments
gone wrong, poison gas clouds released,
whole incorporated areas nothing more than
craters and slurry waste.
Members of your tribe handle snakes.
Swear the track marks on their arms
are part of purity rites, venom injected
to speed revival of sin wracked souls.
Cultivate a look that suggests arc welding
flames spreading from one eye to the next
causing all who see them to squint as if they
were standing too close to a source of
radiant light and pure.
Articulation is like speaking while swimming
underwater without gear, a series of guttural
sounds produced by sound distortion machines,
almost comprehensible but always something
missing that makes the words adhere with
meaning.
At night they lie down to sleep where the
ambulances go to die, bleeding ears infected
by new kinds of ambient noise.
After the last power source fails, the only
light is from their snake skinned eyes glowing
like radiant heat fireflies driven mad
by the heat.

Play It as It Lays

After she'd slept with all
the summer clubmen and
their able-bodied hangers-on,
there was nothing to do and
endless weeks ahead to do it in.

The only one of the so-called
men who had excited her was
a shy, barely verbal, busboy
she'd mercy fucked out of the
goodness of her heart.

Afterwards he'd been unable
to look at her directly, dropped
dishes whenever she was around.
Had become so useless there
was talk of dismissal which
devolved to the level of idle talk
now that ICE had made casual
labor almost impossible to secure.

Even a few hours of restorative
nude sunbathing failed to revive
her as it always had in the past.

Dreamt of speedballs and discos,
eighteen hours of non-stop dancing
totally enthralled by the heat of
the crowd, the sound of the techno.
Lost herself at the rave to end all raves.
The one where the light show at the end
of the mind bent her in ways that could
never be straightened out.

Bring Out Your Dead

They were like creatures from
Defoe: passion players and peasants,
chess masters with no plans,
no boards to play on, yellow
hammered with fatal diseases,
jaundice-colored eyes so polluted
everything they looked at died.

They were plague artists,
lepers without limbs, skin scaled
and withered, mummers without skits,
all of them tricked out with nowhere to go.

They were masters of confusion,
exiled from courts, palaces, pilloried
in village squares: reviled, spit on,
and shunned once they were released,
red masked and flushed by death.

They were daughters of Pandora,
sons of Oedipus, openers of locked
doors with dire Do Not Enter warnings,
drinkers of do not imbibe liquors,
potions that killed, or worse, allowed
you to survive.

They had yellow crosses painted
on their dwellings, signs that appeared
overnight as if by agencies unknown
to man, listened for the carts that came
in fog and smoke-filled mornings,
those tumbrels, piled high with bodies,

and the hoarse voice of the cart man
calling everyone to bring out your dead
but no one ever answers, no one moves.

Winter's Bone

If she actually had a picture
in the high school yearbook,
it would have shown a tall,
maybe one hundred pound,
flat chested girl with a half dozen,
clearly visible, homemade tattoos
suggesting a like amount of ink
in places no one was ever likely to
see this side of an autopsy table.
Where her full name and activities
should have been listed would be
a single phrase in quotes, "Bones".
Activities: None
Awards: None
Voted most likely to die before
the age of 30 of an overdose.
Unanimously.

Ten years later she is still kicking,
barely, though, if anything, she'd
lost weight on her special Organ
Failure Diet that ages one double time,
guarantees hair loss and sallow,
sagging, discolored skin.
She won't smile since she lost
most of her teeth, only opens
her mouth to insert cigarette,
light, inhale, exhale, and repeat when
necessary.

She still hangs by the old
school as that is where her best
customers/ suppliers hang.
Might even have graduated if she'd
actually, like gone to class, as they were
putting everyone through as long as
their names appeared on an attendance
sheet in order to score more state aid.
Everyone is hooked on something
these days.

Body Heat

Oppressive night, so thick
with the heat, air clots in
the lungs, and humidity leaves
a stain on the skin as florid as
a bruise that darkens, then deepens,
as the night goes on and on and on.
Long walks from the overworked
fridge, lose their chill at the lips,
beading, condensation like sweat
bubbles on brown textured glass.
There is no taste to it going down,
is a kind of carbonated pain,
six swallows kill, and then it is time
for another. And another after that.
Drinking solves nothing when sleep
refuses to come. The street hazed
by heavy fog, static haloes of street
lamp light disfigures the pavement
into odd shadows beyond definition.
Lazy eyes droop as the stillness
becomes a weight pressing into
swollen flesh. Somewhere, up the road,
over the hill, sirens; the smell of
something burning, black plumes of
smoke rising from a glowing place
streaked by embers and crackling
light as an animated, nearly silent tableau,
so unreal, even the unmistakable scent
of death that accompanies it fails to
change the presumption that this night
might never end.

Two Lane Blacktop

Blood on the asphalt, shrines by
two lanes like desolation row
tombstones, wooden cross tokens
with mag wheels and car part
extras, dearly beloveds,
faded sprays of plastic flowers,
photos when young, a bride wears
black for no one, a Harley honey
torn tee, a tatter of American flags,
belt buckles and torn leather boots
too stiff to ride now, a shrine of
the blessed virgin mother, primitive cave
paintings inside, death heads with
missing teeth, glow in the dark eye
sockets read, black flags with red roses
rampant, family colors, gang colors,
colors that were and are no more,
desert white cross family
plots for the many who died here,
confederate flags and a suppressed
rebel yell, still lives with no place
left to go.

la vie en rose

In a former life, she imagined
she'd become a rock star like Janis.
An icon with a household name but
Southern Comfort gave her migraines,
beer made her sick as a shit house rat,
and the one time dropping of acid,
made her feel as if her hair was on fire
and her fingers were tongue depressors
that needed to be continually shoved
down her throat. There was a special
place for people like her and it sure
as hell wasn't Cleveland.

Spent six months in an alien nation
called Catatonia where bread
and water was considered fine dining.
When she finally returned to a place
she once called home, everyone asked her
where she'd been and she replied,
"Bergen Belsen."
No one disbelieved her.

The Long Riders

They liked it neat with
Rebel Yell shooter backs,
they said, expecting to get
a laugh.

They usually did.

They had reputations as,
cowboys with a hard on
for the world, that needed
to be upheld.

Fighting was what they
enjoyed most, what they did
best, though they would take
the odd woman if one was
around.

There usually was.

The places they hung out in
always had women who went
for Real Men.

Men who traveled with concealed
weapons, loaded gun racks
and a couple of cases of chilled
Lone Star.

You never knew.

Partying for them was a kind
of religion, was never dull,
was script grist for prime time
TV shows and novels with

names like Midnight Tex
and Living Dead Texas Style.

Swore they had sex with
demons and vampires.

Had the scars to prove it
though the puncture wounds
they were so proud of were
from the business end of a
long handled fork used at
a BBQ gone as wrong as
a cookout could

and the scratches on their backs
were from messing with razor
wire fences on walls they had
no good reason to be trying
to scale.

Every roadhouse along a
hundreds of miles flat line
carried Branch or they'd know
the reason why.

Just put a bottle on the bar,
lay out a long row of Yell
and duck.

That wasn't the name of an
actual drink yet but it would
be soon.

About the Author

Alan Catlin has been publishing in college, university and little magazines since the mid 70s. He can say with complete confidence he is the only poet to ever have published in Street Bagel, Magic Changes, Sink Full of Dishes, Tray Full of Lab Rats, Descant, Puerto del Sol, Hollins Critic, The Literary Review, Wormwood Review and Wordsworth's Socks. He has published over sixty chapbooks and full-length books on a wide variety of subjects ranging from *Bar Wars* (Kindred Spirit Press)*,* to *Effects of Sunlight in the Fog* (Bright Hill Press), to *Walking Among Tombstones in the Fog* (Presa Press), *Self-Portrait of the Artist Afraid of His Self-Portrait* (March Street Press) to *Asylum Garden: after Van Gogh* (Dos Madres).

www.ingramcontent.com/pod-product-compliance
Lightning Source LLC
Chambersburg PA
CBHW070457090426
42735CB00012B/2586